FEBRUARY

Ellen Jackson

Illustrated by
Robin DeWitt and Pat DeWitt

Charlesbridge

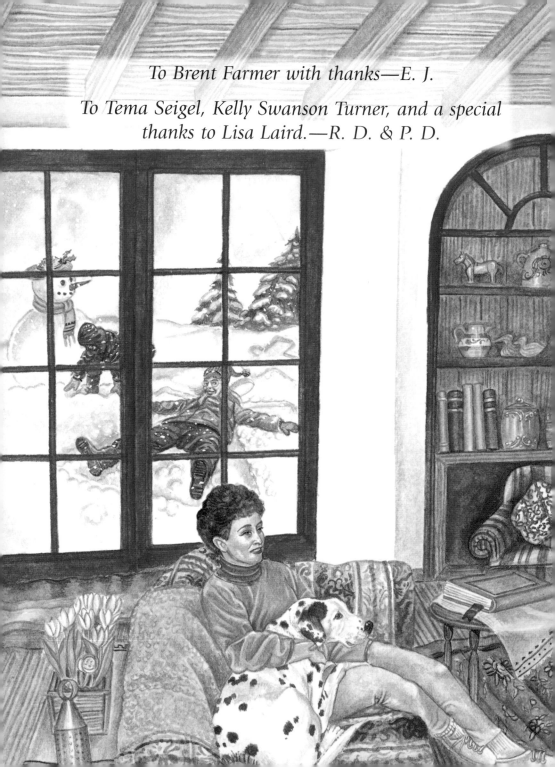

To Brent Farmer with thanks—E. J.

To Tema Seigel, Kelly Swanson Turner, and a special
thanks to Lisa Laird.—R. D. & P. D.

Did You Know?

February is a month of hope. It is a time of icicles and meltwater, violets, and valentines. In the North, February is cold and frosty, and snowdrifts are deeper than at any other time of year. People relax in front of a fireplace and enjoy a bowl of hot oatmeal or a cup of steaming soup. Children bundle up and build snow forts or make angels in the snow.

February may be cold, but a breath of spring is in the air. The black and white shades of January are softening in the winter woods. Poplars show a touch of green, and the tips of willows have a golden glow. The sap in the maples has begun to rise.

Sparrows twitter a few notes, and water trickles beneath the snow. If the weather is mild, people prune trees and clear out brush. In some places, farmers plant potatoes, carrots, and other root crops. An old Arabic proverb says: "Though February storms and blusters, / It has the smell of summer in it."

Because the weather in February can be unpleasant, people who are unhappy are sometimes said to have a "February face." Symbols of Valentine's Day—lacy hearts, ribbons, and candy—are displayed in shop windows. Cupid, a winged child who is full of mischief, is also a Valentine's Day symbol. He is said to shoot arrows at his victims, causing them to fall in love.

In many places, February is a great month for snow sports. Dogsledding, sometimes called mushing, is popular in many northern countries. In 1977, the first Junior Iditarod was held. Young mushers between the ages of fourteen and seventeen competed in a 158-mile dogsled race from Wasilla, just north of Anchorage, to the Yentna Station Roadhouse on the Yentna River. Today, the Junior Iditarod is held in Alaska each February.

Mushing is hard work. Sled dogs do not have
reins like horses, so the musher yells commands to
guide the two lead dogs. Each musher must keep an
eye on the changing weather, the trail conditions,
and the condition of each of the dogs. After the race,
everyone who got to the finish line is honored with
a trophy at a special awards ceremony.

Yentna
Station

The February Birthstone

The birthstone for February is the amethyst, a stone that varies in color from pale violet to deep purple. A Greek myth tells how the god Bacchus poured wine over a maiden named Amethyst, who had been changed into a white stone. The wine turned the stone to purple.

Another legend says that Cleopatra's favorite piece of jewelry was an amethyst ring. Kings and queens of Europe once considered the amethyst a symbol of royalty because only those of royal blood were allowed to wear the color purple.

The February Flower

If you were born in February, your special flower is the violet. The violet is a popular houseplant and garden flower and is found in many parts of the world. In late February, blue, lavender, yellow, or white violets appear in the woods and meadows. The violet was the symbol of ancient Athens, and it is also said to have been the favorite flower of the Islamic prophet Muhammad.

The February Zodiac

Aquarius, the water carrier, is the astrological sign for people with birthdays from January 20 to February 18. People born under Aquarius are able to see both sides of an argument and are good judges of other people. They love nature and are talented in astronomy, science, history, photography, and anything concerned with electricity. But an Aquarius can sometimes daydream a little too much.

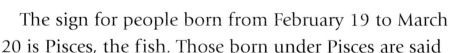

The sign for people born from February 19 to March 20 is Pisces, the fish. Those born under Pisces are said to have great imaginations and to love attention. They always see the good in people. For this reason, they are sometimes too forgiving. A Pisces is also thought to be a good storyteller and a good dancer.

The Calendar

February is the second month of the year. It usually has twenty-eight days, but every fourth year, it has twenty-nine days. The years with extra days are called leap years. Without those extra days, the calendar would gradually become less accurate until it no longer matched the seasons.

The earliest Roman calendar had no official name for the time between December and March. A Roman ruler named Numa Pompilius is credited with dividing this period into two months named *Januarius* and *Februarius*, adding them to the calendar around 700 B.C.

February may take its name from *februare*, a Latin word that means "to purify" or "to cleanse," or from *februa*, the name of a musical instrument that was played at Roman festivals.

Sun, Sky, and Weather

In the woods, the February sun begins to melt the snow, uncovering straw-colored grass from last summer. A few green shoots pop up here and there. Skies are dim, silent, and wrapped in woolly gray.

At night, the aurora borealis, or northern lights, put on a show in the North. Rays of colored light flash silently across the sky. They are caused when particles from the sun strike air molecules high above the surface of the earth near the North Pole.

In late winter, birds have trouble finding food. It is easy to make a February feeder for them. First cut out shapes from slices of bread with a cookie cutter. Then thread a piece of string through a hole in the bread. Spread peanut butter on the bread and cover the peanut butter with sunflower seeds. When you are done, hang the feeder from a fence or a tree.

The Anglo-Saxons, who settled in Britain in the fifth and sixth centuries, called February *Kale monath* because kale, a kind of cabbage, began to grow during this month. The February full moon has been called the snow moon by some Native American peoples, because February is often the month when the snow is deepest.

Animals in February

A February thaw may bring out small insects called snow fleas or springtails. Springtails usually stay hidden beneath dead leaves, but sometimes they come out in huge numbers. In 1993, people in Idaho complained about a "black powder" on the highways. The clean-up team discovered that the powder was made up of millions of these tiny fleas.

In February, male and female red foxes begin to hunt and play together. Soon they will look for a den and wait for their pups to be born. Red foxes will sometimes walk on the thin ice that covers a pond or stream. They seem to know that the surface will not hold a heavier animal that might be following them.

In many places, you can find otter tracks along streams and near ponds. The tracks are easy to spot because of the way the otters bound and slide across the snow. First you will see a set of paw prints, then a place where the snow is pressed flat, then another set of paw prints. Otters hunt small rodents. During the winter, they make holes through the ice of ponds and streams to catch fish.

Some birds are already nesting in February. The great horned owl can be found sitting on her eggs during a snowstorm. After they hatch, the young owls must be fed for nine or ten weeks. Great horned owls sometimes eat porcupines, other owls, and even skunks, which no other animal will eat.

Other birds are enjoying a warmer climate. Most of the world's wild whooping cranes winter along the Gulf Coast of southern Texas. In late February, the birds gain weight to prepare for their long flight north to Canada, where they will nest and lay their eggs. Whooping cranes are the tallest birds in North America. They eat insects, crabs, frogs, rodents, small birds, and berries.

If you live near a wooded area, flying squirrels
may visit your bird feeder in February—especially
if you stock it with sunflower seeds. Flying
squirrels are about as small as chipmunks and are
covered with soft, thick fur. They come out after
dark, but they do not actually fly—they glide,
launching themselves from trees and using their
front legs and tail to steer.

Plants in February

The northeast woods show a hint of spring. A few early flowers, such as the snowdrop, winter aconite, and glory-of-the-snow, bloom before the snow melts. Tiny plants called lichens grow on boulders in bright patches of red, yellow, and apple green.

Oak trees provide shelter and food for many different kinds of animals in late winter. Blue jays, nuthatches, and even bears and raccoons eat the acorns from these trees.

Spruces hold more snow than any other kind of tree, and their branches help break the force of the wind. Many mammals stay near spruce groves in late winter in order to keep warm and take advantage of the shallow snow underneath these trees.

If you live in the city, look for sycamore trees in the park. These trees have beautiful peeling bark that creates patterns of green, white, and tan on their trunks. Seed clusters, called buttonballs, hang from the tips of the branches in February. During a storm, the clusters break apart, and the seeds are swept away by the wind or rain.

In the desert, spring begins in February. This is a good month to visit the Petrified Forest National Park in Arizona. About 225 million years ago, a forest of tall pine trees grew alongside a network of streams. Some of these trees fell into the streams and were carried by floods to their present location. There they were covered with mud, silt, and volcanic ash. Little by little, minerals replaced much of the woody material. Today the logs have completely petrified, or turned to stone.

Special Days

Groundhog Day

Groundhog Day, celebrated in the United States on February 2 each year, is based on an old superstition. The superstition says that if a groundhog sees its shadow early in the morning on Groundhog Day, it will go back to its burrow, and winter weather will continue for six more weeks. But if the groundhog's shadow is not visible, the groundhog will begin its springtime activities, and the worst of winter will be over.

The most famous groundhog is Punxsutawney Phil, who lives in the town of Punxsutawney, Pennsylvania. The head of the Punxsutawney Groundhog Club is said to talk to Phil in groundhog language on February 2. Of course, most people do not really believe that groundhogs can talk or predict the weather. Groundhog Day is just for fun.

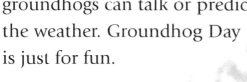

St. Valentine's Day

Everybody likes to get valentines on Valentine's Day, a holiday that has been celebrated on February 14 for centuries. Valentine's Day may have been named for St. Valentine, a Christian who was executed by the Romans around A.D. 270. It is said that before St. Valentine was executed, he made friends with the daughter of the jailor and wrote her a note, signing it "Your Valentine."

Some people send cards decorated with hearts and ribbons to their loved ones on February 14. It is a day to tell everyone you like—friends, neighbors, and family—that they are special and important to you.

Presidents' Day

Presidents' Day is celebrated in the United States on the third Monday in February. On this day, Americans honor two of their greatest presidents, George Washington and Abraham Lincoln.

George Washington, born on February 22, 1732, was the first president of the United States. He was also commander in chief of the Revolutionary army in the War of Independence. Without Washington, the United States of America might not exist.

Born on February 12, 1809, Abraham Lincoln was the sixteenth president of the United States. He held office during the Civil War and is remembered as the president who freed African Americans from slavery. Lincoln was also known for his honesty, modesty, and sense of humor. He was a powerful speaker and writer whose words are often quoted today.

Famous February Events

On February 1, 1709, an English ship rescued Alexander Selkirk after he had spent four years on an uninhabited island off the coast of Chile. He shared the island with goats, wild cats, sea lions, and rats. To survive, he ate fish, turtles,  goats' milk, and cabbage palm. Selkirk's story inspired Daniel Defoe to write *Robinson Crusoe.*

On February 21, 1804, Richard Trevithick ran the first steam-powered railway train between the villages of Penydarren and Abercynon in Wales. Trevithick had been experimenting with his locomotive for months. On its historic first run, the 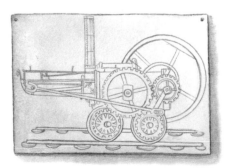 locomotive pulled carriages holding seventy men and moved ten tons of iron. It traveled nine and one-half miles in a little more than two hours.

On February 20, 1962, John Glenn became the first American to orbit the earth. The three-orbit flight, made in the capsule *Friendship 7*, covered a distance of eighty-one thousand miles. Glenn, who was one of the first seven American astronauts, had flown 149 combat missions in World War II and the Korean War. In 1957, he became the first man to make a nonstop supersonic flight from Los Angeles to New York, covering the distance in three hours and twenty-three minutes in an F8U Crusader.

Birthdays

Many famous people were born in February.

Elizabeth Blackwell

February 3, 1821

First woman to graduate from medical school and practice medicine in the United States.

Charles Lindbergh

February 4, 1902

American aviator and first person to fly solo and nonstop over the Atlantic Ocean.

Rosa Parks

February 4, 1913

Civil-rights leader. Her actions led to the 1955 bus boycott in Montgomery, Alabama.

George Herman Ruth

February 6, 1895

Better known as Babe Ruth. Record-breaking baseball player who hit 714 home runs in the major leagues.

Ronald Reagan

February 6, 1911

Fortieth president of the United States and former movie actor.

Thomas Edison

February 11, 1847

Inventor of the electric lamp and the phonograph and holder of 1,093 patents.

Charles Darwin

February 12, 1809

Naturalist and author of *On the Origin of Species*, a book about evolution.

Galileo Galilei

February 15, 1564

Italian astronomer, physicist, and builder of the first useful telescope.

Toni Morrison

February 18, 1931

Nobel Prize-winning novelist best known for the novels *Beloved* and *Sula*.

Marian Anderson

February 27, 1897

Singer and first African American to perform with the New York Metropolitan Opera.

A February Myth

Once, long ago, when birds could talk, two flocks of swans waited impatiently for the arrival of spring.

"Let us go now," said the leader of one flock. "I want to see the northern country. I miss the lakes, the long sunlit days, and the green meadows."

"It is only February," said the leader of the other flock. "The lakes are still covered with ice. The grass sparkles with frost, and the sun is pale and cold. It is not yet time for the great melting, and it is much too early for our journey."

But the first flock would not wait. With a great flapping of wings, one hundred swans rose into the air, heading north at the first blush of dawn. As the swans made their way farther and farther north, they felt the air grow colder.

By the next day, the birds were weary and chilled to the bone. But they would not stop or turn back. That night, they flew into an ice storm and froze in the sky. And that is where they are to this day. Now and then, some of them will flutter a bit, and light is reflected from their wings.

The people of Scandinavia have a name for this soft flickering. They call it the aurora borealis, or northern lights.

AUTHOR'S NOTE

This book gives an overview of the month of February in North America. But nature does not follow a strict schedule. The mating and migration of animals, the blooming of plants, and other natural events vary from year to year, or occur earlier or later in different places.

The zodiac sections of this book are included just for fun as part of the folklore of the month and should not be taken as accurate descriptions of any real people.

The February story was adapted from *Spirits of the Wild: The World's Great Nature Myths* by Gary Ferguson (New York: Three Rivers Press, 1996.)

Text copyright © 2002 by Ellen Jackson
Illustrations copyright © 2002
  by Robin DeWitt and Pat DeWitt
All rights reserved, including the right of
  reproduction in whole or in part in any form.
The illustrations of John Glenn on page 27 are
  based on photographs © NASA.

Published by Charlesbridge Publishing
85 Main Street, Watertown, MA 02472
(617) 926-0329
www.charlesbridge.com

Illustrations done in watercolor on Arches
  hot-press paper
Display type and text type set in Giovanni
Color separations made by Sung In Printing,
  South Korea
Printed and bound by Sung In Printing,
  South Korea
Production supervision by Brian G. Walker
Designed by Diane M. Earley

**Library of Congress
Cataloging-in-Publication Data**

Jackson, Ellen B., 1943-
  February/Ellen Jackson; illustrated by
  Robin DeWitt and Pat DeWitt.
    p. cm.—(It happens in the month of)
  ISBN 0-88106-996-5 (hardcover)
  1. February—Folklore. 2. February—
  Juvenile literature. [1. February.] I. DeWitt,
  Robin, ill. II. DeWitt, Pat, ill. III. Title.

GR930.J333   2002
398'.33—dc21   2001028266

Printed in South Korea
10 9 8 7 6 5 4 3 2 1